Publisher Notes:

Cataloging-in-Public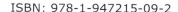
may be obtained fr

ISBN: 978-1-947215-09-2

An imprint of Activity Giants, LLC

Activity Giants, LLC books are available at special discounts when purchased in quantity for premiums and promotions as well as fundraising or educational use. Special editions can also be created to specification. For details contact info@activitygiants.com or the address below:

Activity Giants
PO BOX 531412 Henderson, NV 89052
www.activitygiants.com

Q: What's the Easter Bunny's favorite restaurant?

A: IHOP!

Q: Why are Easter Bunnys so lucky?

A: They each have four rabbits feet!

Q: What music does the Easter Bunny listen to?

A: Hip-Hop!

Q. Why was the Easter Bunny so upset?

A. He was having a bad hare day!

Q. Why shouldn't you tell an Easter egg a good joke?

A. It might crack up!

Q. What did one colored egg say to the other?

A. Heard any good yolks lately?

Q. What kind of beans never grow in a garden?

A. Jelly beans!

Q. How did the soggy Easter Bunny dry himself?

A. With a hare dryer!

Q. How does the Easter bunny stay in shape?

A. Lots of eggs-ercise!

Q. What do you call a dumb bunny?

A. A hare brain.

Q. What's the best way to catch a unique rabbit?

A. Unique up on him.

Q. How do you catch a tame rabbit?

A. Tame way, unique up on it.

Q. Why can't a rabbit's nose be twelve inches long?

A. Because then it would be a foot.

Q. How can you tell which rabbits are the oldest in a group?

A. Just look for the gray hares.

Q. What do you call a line of rabbits walking backwards?

A. A receding hareline.

Q. How do you know carrots are good for your eyes?

A. Have you ever seen a rabbit with glasses?

Q. What do you call a rabbit who tells jokes?

A. A funny bunny.

Q. What is a rabbit's favorite dance?

A. The Bunny Hop.

Q. What kind of jewelry do rabbits wear?

A. 14 carrot gold.

Q. What do you call a rabbit with fleas?

A. Bugs Bunny.

Q. Why did the Easter egg hide?

A. He was a little chicken.

Q. How do rabbits say good-bye to carrots?

A. It's been nice gnawing you!

Q: How does a rabbit make gold soup?

A: He begins with 24 carrots.

Q: What do you get when you cross a bunny with a spider?

A: A harenet.

Q. Why does the Easter bunny have a shiny nose?

A. His powder puff is on the wrong end.

Q. What is the difference between a crazy bunny and a counterfeit banknote?

A. One is bad money and the other is a mad bunny!

Q. Why is a bunny the luckiest animal in the world?

A. It has four rabbits' feet.

Q. What do you get when you cross a bunny with an onion?

A. A bunion.

Q. What do you get when you pour hot water down a rabbit hole?

A. A hot cross bunny.

Q: When is an elephant like the Easter Bunny?

A: When he's wearing his Easter Bunny suit.

Q: What do you call a chocolate Easter bunny out in the sun too long?

A: A runny bunny.

Q: Why couldn't the rabbit fly home for Easter?

A: He didn't have the hare fare.

Q: How many chocolate bunnies can you put into an empty Easter basket?

A: One. After that the basket won't be empty.

Q: Why did the rabbit cross the road?

A: Because the chicken had his Easter eggs.

Q: Where do Easter bunnies dance?

A: At the basketball.

Q. What do you get if you pour hot water down a rabbit hole?

A. Hot cross bunnies!

Q. What do you call a rabbit with fleas?

A. Bugs Bunny!

Q. Why shouldn't you tell an Easter egg a joke?

A. It might crack up!

Q. How did the soggy Easter Bunny dry himself?

A. With a hare-dryer!

Q. Why did the Easter Bunny cross the road?

A. Because the chicken had his Easter eggs!

Q. What did the rabbit say to the carrot?

A. It's been nice gnawing you!

Q. How did the Easter Bunny rate the Easter parade?

A. He said it was eggs-cellent!

Q. How does the Easter Bunny travel?

A. By hare-plane!

Q. How does the Easter Bunny stay fit?

A. Eggs-ercise and hare-robics!

Q. What happened when the Easter Bunny met the rabbit of his dreams?

A. They lived hoppily ever after!

Made in the USA
Middletown, DE
17 April 2019